PRIMARY SOURCES OF THE THIRTEEN COLONIES AND THE LOST COLONY ™

A Primary Source History of the Colony of
VIRGINIA

SANDRA WHITEKNACT

rosen central
Primary Source™

The Rosen Publishing Group, Inc., New York

For Helen Jones Hinton (1925-2003) and Ronda Jones Levin

Published in 2006 by The Rosen Publishing Group, Inc.
29 East 21st Street, New York, NY 10010

Library of Congress Cataloging-in-Publication Data

Whiteknact, Sandra.
A primary source history of the colony of Virginia/Sandra Whiteknact.—1st ed.
    p. cm.—(Primary sources of the thirteen colonies and the lost colony)
Includes bibliographical references and index.
ISBN 1-4042-0437-7 (lib. bdg.)
ISBN 1-4042-0678-7 (pbk. bdg.)
1. Virginia—History—Colonial period, ca. 1600-1775—Juvenile literature. 2. Virginia—History—Colonial period, ca. 1600-1775—Sources—Juvenile literature.
I. Title. II. Series.
F229.W577 2006
975.5'02—dc22

2004030300

Manufactured in the United States of America

On the cover: Engraving by Theodor de Bry (1528–1598) entitled *Captain Gosnold Trades with the Indians.*

CONTENTS

INTRODUCTION

W e hold these truths to be self-evident, that all men are created equal, that they are endowed by their Creator with certain inalienable Rights, that among these are life, liberty, and the pursuit of happiness."

You probably recognize the words above. They are from the American Declaration of Independence, adopted by the members of the Continental Congress in Philadelphia, Pennsylvania, on July 4, 1776. For many Americans, past and present, the words quoted above are a fundamental statement of the most important American values.

From Virginians to Americans

What the declaration says is that these rights—freedom and equality being the most important among them—belong to every individual simply by the fact of their being born. These rights, the declaration says, are "inalienable"— they are not given by a king or granted by a government. They belong to each individual as surely as that person's life belongs to him or her. Moreover, they cannot be taken away.

It would perhaps be easy to take these words for granted today, for it is hard for anyone today to realize how truly revolutionary they were at the time they were written. Those who signed the declaration believed that the "truths" it stated were "self-evident," or obvious. Yet, in 1776, there was not a true democracy on the face of the earth. There was also not a single society that in any way could have claimed to be based on such principles as freedom and equality. The people of Great Britain prided themselves on being free men and women, but very few among them would have argued that the members of their society were equal. In fact, very few among them would even have agreed that equality in a society was a realistic goal or even one that was worth pursuing. To such people, the very idea of a true democracy was frightening. It meant mob rule, disorder, chaos, and anarchy.

The person who wrote the bold, revolutionary words on the previous page was Thomas Jefferson. Jefferson was a Virginian, like many of the leading figures at the Continental Congress. Not even Pennsylvania, the largest colony, could claim a leadership role as great as Virginia's; only Massachusetts was nearly as influential. Besides Jefferson, George Washington, a Virginian, was commander in chief of the Continental army. Patrick Henry, a Virginian, was a fiery orator and a delegate to the congress whose famous declaration "Give me liberty, or give me death" had become a rallying cry for the American patriots. James Madison, a Virginian, would write much of the Constitution, including the Bill of Rights. He also wrote many of the Federalist Papers, which helped convince Americans to make the Constitution the law of their new nation. Four of the first five presidents of the new nation of the United States—Washington, Jefferson, Madison, and James Monroe—were Virginians. The first great chief justice of the Supreme Court, John Marshall, was also a Virginian.

Yet, even earlier in their own lifetimes, these men would not have thought of themselves as Americans, nor would have most of their fellow colonists. First and foremost, they would have considered themselves Virginians. They also would have thought themselves to have relatively little in common with the residents of the other American colonies. Even other delegates at the

Pictured here are three Virginians who would serve as president of the United States, among many other great accomplishments: *(clockwise from left)* George Washington, James Madison, and Thomas Jefferson. All three Virginians were born into distinguished tobacco planter families. Washington's lasting legacy was his peaceful relinquishing of power when he turned down serving more than a second term as president. Madison was an advocate of limiting the power of the federal government and basing state representation on population. Jefferson's vision for the United States was as an agricultural nation.

Continental Congress commented on the lordly, even arrogant manner with which the Virginians carried themselves. Similarly, they, and most certainly their parents before them, would have considered themselves British subjects, not American citizens. They would have been proud of their British heritage, considering themselves free British gentlemen, and most likely would have considered that to be the central element of their identity.

Likewise, it would have required a great leap forward in consciousness for any of them to conceive of a society based on equality. Their wealth and status, as well as the economy of Virginia, was based on a system rooted in the most fundamental inequality and lack of freedom—slavery. Their forefathers would likely have left Great Britain to come to Virginia not because it was a place where they could achieve equality, but because it was a place where they had a chance to wind up on top in the social and economic order of things.

So what happened that made Virginians such as George Washington, Thomas Jefferson, James Madison, and Patrick Henry take such a different view of themselves and their colony? The answer to that question is in the story of the colony of Virginia.

CHAPTER 1

For Gold, for Praise, for Glory

At the beginning of the seventeenth century, England was in the midst of one of the most dynamic periods in its history. The death of Queen Elizabeth I in 1603 marked the end of forty-five years of her remarkable reign.

Elizabeth had taken the throne of England in 1558. She was the daughter of King Henry VIII. Henry had married six different women, executed two of them, and created a schism between England and the Roman Catholic Church in his determination to father a son to succeed him on England's throne.

A New Church

Henry feared that a daughter would be an insufficiently strong leader to keep the throne in the face of challenges. When Henry's first wife did not bear him a son, the king sought a divorce. However, Roman Catholicism prevented divorce. When the pope, the head of the Roman Catholic Church, refused to grant permission to Henry to marry again, Henry rejected the pope's authority and declared himself the head of a new English church, the Church of England. England, therefore, came down on the Protestant side of the Reformation, as the religious upheaval then taking place in Europe would come to be known.

All of the English people, however, were not as quick as Henry to reject Catholicism and embrace Protestantism. This was despite various laws providing for the punishment and persecution of those who continued in Catholic belief and practice. As on the European

Mary I *(left)* was the daughter of King Henry VIII and Catherine of Aragon. It was from Catherine that Henry sought a divorce in order to marry Anne Boleyn in his desperation for a male heir. However, this desperation was not immediate upon Mary's birth. Instead, it happened nearly twenty years later when it became apparent that Mary would be his sole offspring. Anne Boleyn was the mother of Queen Elizabeth I *(right)*. Queen Mary's rule was considered tragic, but her half sister Elizabeth's rule is considered England's golden age.

continent, the Reformation in England was thus also characterized by a bloody struggle between Protestants and Catholics.

Succession and Religious Strife

Upon his death in 1547, Henry was succeeded by his sole son, Edward, who ruled as King Edward VI. Edward was a Protestant determined to root out Catholicism in England. Yet he was a sickly young man who ruled only six years before dying. Edward was followed as monarch by another of Henry's children,

This is a page from *Die Societas Jesu in Europa*, 1643 to 1644, engraved by Mathias Tanner. The engraving depicts Jesuit priest Brian Cansfield being attacked by English Protestant authorities in Yorkshire, England. Cansfield was then imprisoned and died from the results of the cruelty on August 3, 1643. The Jesuit order is a religious order of the Catholic Church, devoted to missionary work and education.

Mary Tudor, destined to be remembered in English history as Bloody Mary. Mary was a Roman Catholic, which meant that it was now English Protestants who had to fear for their life and property.

Traitors or Martyrs

It was on Mary's death in 1558 that Elizabeth took the throne. Elizabeth was a Protestant, however, and now it was Catholics who had to go into hiding or exile or renounce their faith. At the time, religious belief in England was a matter of political loyalty; to profess the "wrong" faith was considered treason. Whether one believed the persecuted to be traitors or martyrs depended on one's point of view and sympathies.

The Geneva Bible was England's most popular Bible from 1560 to 1644. English reformers who had settled in Geneva, Switzerland, after escaping the persecution of Queen Mary translated this Bible. The Puritans and Pilgrims first brought the Geneva Bible to the New World. The King James Bible gradually replaced the Geneva Bible as the most popular version. However, the theology in the Geneva Bible would influence the settling of America.

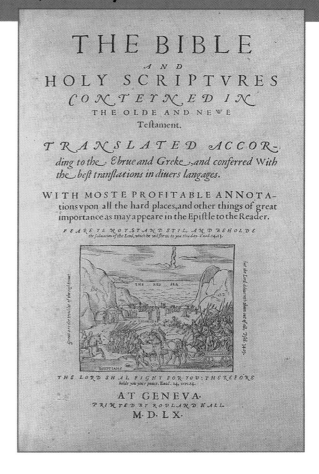

Elizabeth proved to be a strong and extremely capable ruler. However, that never lessened the fear of disloyalty and rebellion that Catholicism provoked. Elizabeth's secret agents, the "searchers," were constantly uncovering rumors of plots by English Catholics in league with agents of the Catholic nations of France and Spain. In the first decades of Elizabeth's reign, Catholics were also always feared to be conspiring to rise up and put Elizabeth's Catholic cousin, the beautiful Mary, Queen of Scots, on the throne of England. In response, on the advice of her advisers, Elizabeth had Mary imprisoned and ultimately beheaded.

The sense of security of England's Protestant nobility and royalty was not lessened by Pope Pius V's decision in 1570 to excommunicate, or formally expel, Elizabeth from the Roman Catholic Church. The pope's order of excommunication also stated that all faithful English Catholics should consider themselves forbidden to obey Elizabeth or any of the laws of her kingdom. In 1580, Pope Gregory XIII added that any Catholic who assassinated Queen Elizabeth would not be committing a sin.

Grim Reprisals

In response, Elizabeth's government instituted ever-stronger measures against English Catholics. The Catholic Mass was made illegal, and attendance at Protestant religious services was made mandatory, under penalty of a heavy fine or even imprisonment. Becoming a Catholic priest was made illegal, as was knowing, protecting, or sheltering a Catholic priest or possessing traditional Catholic religious items, such as a crucifix, rosary, religious medallion, or pictures of the saints.

Punishment of Catholic "traitors" caught by the searchers was gruesomely severe, intended to leave terror in the hearts of anyone tempted to behave similarly. Typically, Catholics convicted of conspiring against the British crown were hideously tortured until they confessed, then dragged through the muddy streets of London tied to a wooden frame pulled by a horse to Tyburn, the place of public execution. There, while huge crowds watched and jeered, they were hanged from the gallows, then cut down while still alive so that they could be tortured some more. Then, as the traitors still clung to life, their intestines were pulled out and burned in front of them. Finally, mercifully, they were beheaded and their bodies drawn and quartered, or cut into four pieces. The pieces were then displayed from some of the hundreds of gibbets on the outskirts of London, while their heads, if they were deemed important enough, would be displayed from pikes on London Bridge.

A Catholic Enemy

Religion also now came to play a role in England's foreign affairs. Its greatest rival was staunchly Catholic Spain, the richest and strongest power in Europe. Spain's riches resulted from the "discovery" of the New World by Christopher Columbus. Following Columbus's landing on the Caribbean island of Hispaniola in 1492, thousands of Spanish conquistadores and colonists sailed for the New World.

A Disease of the Heart

Back in Spain, Columbus had been ridiculed because his discoveries did not yield great riches in the form of gold and silver, but the Spanish who followed were more fortunate. In 1519, in what is now Mexico, the Spanish conquistador Hernán Cortés conquered the wealthy and powerful empire of the Aztec people, whose capital city, Tenochtitlán, was larger, richer, and possibly more beautiful than anything in Europe. Fifteen years later, another Spanish conqueror, Francisco Pizarro, triumphed over an equally wealthy Native American people, the Incas of the Andes Mountains of Peru. Both of these empires had access to rich mines of gold and silver.

Gold and silver "is certainly something for which [the Spanish] yearn with a great thirst," the Aztecs wrote in the *Florentine Codex*, accounts of the Spanish conquest compiled by Spanish priests after the fact. "Their bodies fatten on it and they hunger violently for it. They crave gold like hungry swine." Cortés, for one, essentially agreed with the Aztec assessment. "We Spanish have a disease of the heart that can only be cured by gold," Cortés told the Aztecs, according to the recollections of his secretary, Francisco Lopez de Gomara, in his *General History of the Indies with the Conquest of Mexico and New Spain.* And in the islands of the Caribbean and in Brazil, the Spanish and their Iberian neighbors, the Portuguese, also discovered that the New World was ideal for the cultivation of a crop that was worth its weight in gold—sugar.

Worth a Peru

In a short time, New World gold, silver, and sugar made Spain the richest nation in Europe. "Worth a Peru" became the ultimate accolade of value and wealth. Spain's new wealth stimulated the European economy as well. Ships and merchants from the nations of Europe flocked to Spain's ports and countinghouses to sell various goods that Spain's new wealth enabled Spain to buy. A French government official even remarked how the more nations did business with Spain, the more wealth those nations would have.

Spain also saw godly work in its discovery. After much debate, the Catholic Church declared that the native peoples of the New World, in fact, possessed souls, just like Europeans. This meant that it was the obligation of the native peoples' new Spanish rulers to claim these souls for Roman Catholicism. Conquest and religious conversion went hand in hand in the Spanish territories of the New World.

Preying on Spain

England's rulers watched these developments with great interest. For a time, England was neither wealthy enough nor sufficiently strong enough militarily to directly challenge Spain for colonies

This is a depiction of the fort of Saint Augustine under Sir Francis Drake's attack on May 28 and 29, 1586. Baptista Boazio, an Italian mapmaker who was located in London from 1585 to 1603, created a series of maps to depict Drake's expedition to the West Indies. The fort came under attack by Drake, who looted and burned the settlement and then sailed northward, stopping by the Roanoke settlement on his way back to England. This hand-colored engraving also depicts a dolphin, most likely copied from a John White drawing that Boazio had seen.

in the New World. Initially, England benefited from New World trade primarily through the use of privateers. A privateer was an armed private ship given permission by the British crown to attack and raid the shipping of other nations. The captain of the privateer was allowed to keep whatever plunder it obtained from such raids after paying the British crown its required share.

Essentially, privateers were pirates commissioned by the government to act as such. The greatest English naval hero of the Elizabethan age, Sir Francis Drake, made his fortune and reputation as a privateer preying on Spanish shipping and New World colonial settlements. Obviously, the profit motive was a powerful incentive. The British were also motivated by national pride and religious sentiment, believing that in thwarting Spain, they were doing God's work by halting the spread of Catholicism.

English confidence grew throughout Elizabeth's reign, peaking in 1588. In that year, Spain assembled the largest naval expedition in history to attack and invade England, but the Spanish Armada, as it was known, was defeated by a combination of bad weather and Drake's naval genius.

Gold, Praise, and Glory

English mariners and adventurers were now eager to establish New World colonies of their own. As Sir Walter Raleigh, who was one of those encouraging Elizabeth to embark on colonial adventures in the New World, put it, it had become clear "that he who commands the sea, commands the trade, and he that is Lord of the Trade of the World is lord of the wealth of the world, and consequently of the world itself." England hoped to profit financially from colonies. It would also benefit spiritually, by introducing the people it conquered to the "true religion" of Protestant Christianity. It was time, Raleigh explained, for England "to seek new worlds for gold, for praise, for glory."

CHAPTER 2

As the English ruling classes saw it, colonization of the New World could be made to serve yet one more purpose: disposing of England's "surplus population." England was in the midst of a population explosion. Between 1500 and 1600, the population of England had increased from 3 million to 4 million people. In the next fifty years, the population would grow by another million, to 5 million.

Masterless Men and Sturdy Beggars

For the British upper class, the increased population represented a threat. Although the English prided themselves on being the freest people in the world, theirs was far from being a democratic society. Nor was it based in any way on equality.

Aristocrats and Gentry

About 5 percent of the English population consisted of what was known as the aristocracy or the gentry. The aristocracy consisted of those nobles—dukes, barons, lords, and knights—who had inherited property and a title. The gentry were those who had managed to accumulate some property and the status that went with it, despite not being born into the aristocracy.

The aristocracy was represented in the British government by the House of Lords, the upper house of Parliament, as Britain's lawmaking body was known. One inherited one's seat in the House of Lords the same way one inherited a noble title.

The gentry, or "middling classes," were represented by the House of Commons. Members of the House of Commons were

Sir Thomas Smythe was an entrepreneur who, in 1588, helped finance and raise the funds necessary for the English fleet to defeat the Spanish Armada. In 1609, he acquired the charter to the Virginia Company and served as treasurer until 1618, when he was falsely accused of embezzlement. Nevertheless, Smythe is largely credited for the success of the Virginia colony.

elected by the people, but only male property owners had the right to vote. Only about 25 percent of adult British males owned enough property to qualify to vote under these standards.

Vagrants and Vagabonds

That left about 95 percent of the rapidly growing British population without property or political rights. Most of the members of these lower classes were agricultural laborers on land owned by the nobility or gentry. Or, they were urban workers in cities like London, the population of which was growing almost as fast as all of England's. The trouble was that these populations were growing too fast to keep all these people in work and thereby fed, clothed, satisfied, and at home. Those without work often took to the roads to find it, wandering from country estate to country

This woodcut depicts a beggar tied and whipped by local authorities through the cobblestone streets of London, circa 1567. The population of London had grown from 120,000 in 1550 to 200,000 in 1600. London's reputation was one of crime, poverty, filth, plagues, and fires, as well as of execution. The form of punishment shown here had been approved by Parliament in response to the growing problem of wandering vagrants who caused anxiety to the ruling class. There was fear that the growing number of the impoverished would cause the collapse of a stable society.

estate or making their way to London, which drew the restless and dissatisfied to it like a huge magnet.

These wanderers greatly disturbed the authorities, who saw them as signs of incipient disorder and possible harbingers of unrest and political agitation. Legislation was passed against these sturdy beggars or masterless men, as these able-bodied men without work were called. Virtually all travel in pursuit of "legitimate" business required licenses. Vagrancy—to be without any visible means of support or fixed address—was made a crime. By the terms of the Vagabond Act of 1604, for example, any stranger found wandering the roads could be arrested and brought to the

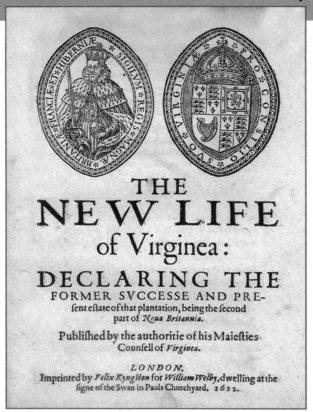

THE
NEW LIFE
of Virginea:

DECLARING THE
FORMER SVCCESSE AND PRE-
sent estate of that plantation, being the second
part of Noua Britannia.

Published by the authoritie of his Maiesties
Counsell of Virginea.

LONDON,
Imprinted by Felix Kyngston for William Welby, dwelling at the
signe of the Swan in Pauls Churchyard. 1612.

Shown here is the title page of the book *The New Life of Virginea*, which was the sequel to a previously published discourse on the excellent opportunities that planting in Virginia offered. The goal of *The New Life*, published in 1612 in London, was to entice immigrants to Virginia, which was beginning to flourish at this time. See the transcription of this image on page 54.

authorities for interrogation. If the "vagabond" could not show that he owned property or was serving a "master" who did, he could be publicly whipped, returned to his place of birth, or jailed until someone would provide him with work. Similar legislation allowed vagrants to be whipped and sold into slavery.

The Gallows

Poverty and unemployment naturally led to increased crime, particularly theft. The upper classes were merciless in punishing such crimes against property, making theft equal to murder as capital crimes punishable by hanging. In seventeenth-century England, there were no less than 200 crimes, most of them against property, that were punishable as hanging offenses.

Even those with a place to live and work to do began to suffer. The growing number of unemployed and poverty-stricken people meant greater competition for what work was available. This allowed employers to cut what wages they did pay, since it was easy to find someone who would work for whatever wage was offered. At the same time, increasing demand drove up the cost of food and housing. The result was that between 1500 and 1650, real wages for England's working classes fell by half.

Enclosure

At the same time, in the countryside, noble landowners were trying to extract more wealth from their lands. One result was enclosure—the fencing in of the forest and pasture lands of the great estates. Traditionally, the rural, landless poor had relied on these lands to hunt on, graze animals, and gather roots, herbs, and plants to use as food and medicine. The enclosure movement meant even more hardship for the rural poor and sent even more of them on the road as sturdy beggars and masterless men.

By the seventeenth century, much of the ruling class in England had begun to see colonization of the New World as a possible solution for the problem of surplus population. Despite the presence of Native Americans, North America, as they saw it, was a land of unlimited empty space that needed to be populated and worked.

North America might prove to be little more than a "howling wilderness," as some in England called it, but many would still want to go there, out of a desire for greater opportunity than any they would ever have in England. Even more could be made to go there as an alternative to imprisonment or forced servitude. The masterless men and sturdy beggars who were plaguing England would make the perfect labor force for the New World.

CHAPTER 3

Plantation or Slaughterhouse

The area that the English colonizers had in mind for the first British colony in North America lay about halfway down the continent's eastern seaboard, on the western shore of a huge irregularly shaped body of water known as the Chesapeake Bay. The English called this land Virginia, in honor of Queen Elizabeth, who was referred to as "the virgin queen" because she never married.

Roanoke

In 1585, Sir Walter Raleigh made the first attempt at establishing an English colony in this region when he dispatched 108 settlers, all of them men, to a small island called Roanoke on the Outer Banks of present-day North Carolina. It proved to be a poor choice for a first settlement. Long sandbanks and treacherous shoals guarded the island, making it difficult for ships to approach. Roanoke's soil also proved poor for growing crops, as it was too sandy.

The would-be colonists also proved poor for growing crops. Most apparently believed that they were going to strike it rich in the New World by finding gold and silver. They were reluctant to do the hard work of clearing fields, planting and harvesting crops, or even hunting.

Instead, they assumed that the Native American population of the region could be made to feed them. The Native Americans were used to growing, gathering, and hunting enough food only to feed their people. The unexpected burden of providing for

Artist John White accompanied Sir Walter Raleigh on his 1585 voyage to the New World. He created more than seventy watercolor drawings of the Native Americans, animals, and plants he encountered at Roanoke. At left is the Indian village of Pomeiooc. Private dwellings, common areas, and public buildings were typical of native villages. Several houses are depicted with the exteriors removed to show the interiors. The elaborate body paint of the Native American at right indicates he was perhaps preparing for a hunting expedition. He is armed with a bow and a basket of arrows. He also sports what might possibly be a puma's tail, attached to the backside of his garment.

more than 100 less-than-welcome newcomers soon proved intolerable. When, by the spring of 1586, the Native Americans began to be reluctant to supply the colonists with food, the colonists attacked the local villages without warning, killing several chiefs. In response, the Native Americans simply fled the area, leaving the colonists even less able to provide for themselves. When English ships called at Roanoke later that spring, all of the surviving colonists took the opportunity to return to England.

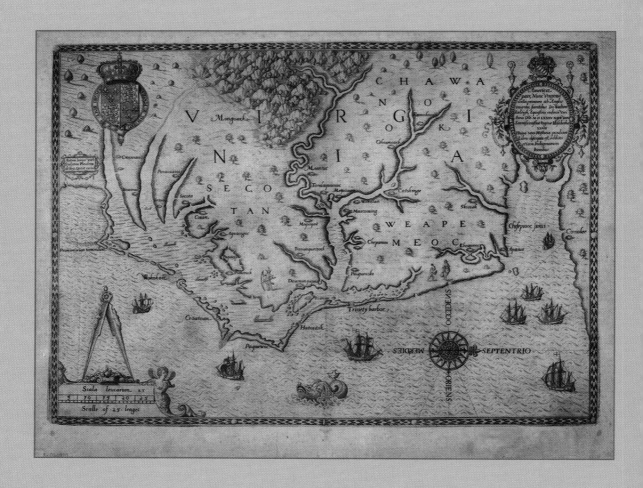

This map, engraved by Theodor de Bry and based on drawings by John White, was published in Frankfurt, Germany in 1590. It is the first printed map specifically of Virginia (the coastal region of present-day North Carolina). The map covers from Chesapeake Bay to Cape Lookout. It includes English ships approaching the outer banks, a sea monster, Britain's royal arms, and a navigational compass. A number of dugout canoes with their native inhabitants can be seen in Pamlico and Ablemarle sounds. Roanoke (spelled here as "Roanoac") is the small island north of "Hatorask" and south of the mainland.

"Croatoan"

In 1587, Raleigh tried again. By now, he recognized that Roanoke was a poor site for a colony. This time, he intended for his group of 117 colonists, including seventeen women and nine children, to settle along the Chesapeake Bay. The captain of the ships transporting the colonists had different ideas, however. Eager to get to the Caribbean and prey on Spanish shipping, they once again left the colonists at Roanoke.

Again, the colonists proved unwilling or unable to plant crops for themselves, hoping instead to discover a gold mine. The expedition's leader, John White, was forced to sail back to England for more supplies. When he returned to Roanoke in the summer of 1590, he found the colony abandoned and all the colonists vanished. Only the mysterious word "Croatoan" carved into a tree offered any clue as to the fate of the colonists. Exactly what happened to the colonists remains a mystery. The most likely explanation is that hunger and desperation forced them to abandon the colony and that they subsequently joined one of the Native American peoples of the region.

The Bay

For their next attempts in Virginia, the British focused on Chesapeake Bay. For a seafaring people like the British, the Chesapeake region was bound to seem an ideal site for a colony. The Chesapeake Bay is 200 miles (322 kilometers) long and anywhere from 4 to 30 miles (6.4 to 48 km) wide, extending northward from the Atlantic Ocean far inland into what are now the states of Virginia and Maryland.

On its western shore, the Chesapeake is watered by four rivers—the Potomac, the James, the York, and the Rappahannock—

each of them larger than any river in England and all of them navigable at least 100 miles (160 km) inland. Numerous streams and tributaries branch out from these and other smaller rivers, leaving the land along the Chesapeake well watered and fertile. "No country can compare with it [in] number of navigable rivers, creeks and inlets," wrote a seventeenth-century colonist in a report back to England.

The entire coastline of the Chesapeake, on both its western and eastern shores, is jagged with inlets and estuaries. When the English arrived in the Chesapeake region, both shores were covered with unimaginably thick and towering forests. Here, as elsewhere along the Atlantic Coast of North America, sailors were able to detect the scent of pine trees while still 150 miles (241 km) offshore. The trees in these forests reached as tall as 70 feet (21 meters), in enormous variety. Beneath them, wild fruits grew in profusion.

The Virginia Company

According to Captain John Smith in his *Generall Historie of Virginia*, "heaven and earth never agreed better to frame a place for man's habitation" than the Chesapeake Bay. Smith was one of the men chosen by the Virginia Company to lead the new colony it planned to establish in 1607. The Virginia Company was a group of investors and merchants that had received a charter from King James I, Elizabeth's successor, to establish a colony in Virginia. For the next seventeen years, it was the Virginia Company that recruited settlers and distributed land in Virginia. After the company went bankrupt in 1624, Virginia was administered directly by the British crown as a royal colony.

In 1607, three English ships left Smith and 103 others at a location 60 miles (97 km) up the James River from the Chesapeake.

John Smith *(left)* left England in 1596 at age sixteen and volunteered to help the Dutch fight against Spain. Then he joined Austrian forces fighting the Turks in 1600. In 1602 he was captured in Transylvania and sold into slavery to a Turk. He escaped and returned to England in 1604. *The Generall Historie of Virginia, New England, and the Summer Isles (right)*, published in 1624, is his account of his adventures in the New World. Some exaggerated accounts are included. For instance, he describes fighting off 200 Native Americans while using one as a human shield. See transcription on page 54.

Smith wrote that the region was a place of "pleasant plain hills and fertile valleys, one prettily crossing another, and watered so conveniently with their sweet brooks and crystal springs, as if art itself had devised them." The English called their new settlement Jamestown.

The Dying Time

Unfortunately, the region was not healthy—at least not for the English newcomers. Of the 104 first colonists at Jamestown, only

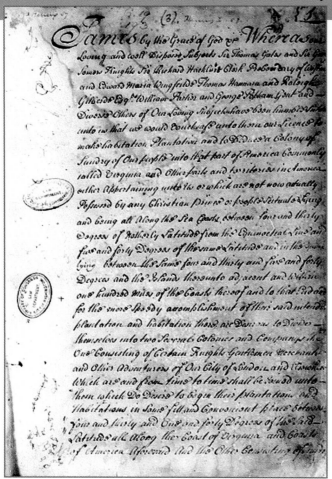

The Virginia Company of London obtained the legal right to start a colony in the New World through a series of charters issued in 1606, 1609, and 1612. The charter of 1606, pictured here, describes the rights of the settlers and outlines the Virginia Company as the "tenant" of the land and the colonists as the sub-tenants of the king's property.

38 were alive nine months later. New shipments of colonists by the Virginia Company raised the colony's population to 220 as of December 1609, but after a brutal winter, only 60 of them were still alive come springtime. Between 1607 and 1622, the Virginia Company shipped 10,000 colonists to Virginia; only 2,000 of them—20 percent—were still alive in 1622.

Although most Virginia colonists regarded the Native Americans as the greatest danger they would face in the New World, disease—malaria, typhus, and dysentery—and hunger were much more likely to carry them off. Many colonists seemed simply to succumb to the climate, which in spring, summer, and fall was unbearably hot and humid for people accustomed to more moderate temperatures.

Indeed, the summer and early fall, when the temperature and humidity tended to be at their highest, was referred to by the colonists as the "dying time." The death rate among the first colonists was so high that an anonymous writer in a pamphlet published in England was moved to comment, "Instead of a plantation, Virginia will shortly get the name of a slaughterhouse."

CHAPTER 4

Despite the obvious difficulties of life there, Virginia continued to attract colonists. Before 1620, most colonists unwillingly came to Virginia, shipped there as unwanted orphans or criminals convicted of vagrancy or theft. After 1620, the majority of Virginia colonists came ostensibly of their own free will,

Second Sons and Distressed Cavaliers

although desperate economic conditions made it questionable as to how much choice they actually had. Of the 120,000 British immigrants to the Chesapeake region in the seventeenth century, 90,000 of them—75 percent— were indentured servants.

Freedom Dues

The vast majority of these colonists were poor people from the south and west of England. Most were sturdy beggars who had left their rural homes to seek work in the cities, especially London. They were offered free transportation to Virginia if they agreed to work there for landowners as unpaid laborers for terms ranging from four to seven years. If they successfully completed this period of forced servitude, they were rewarded with their "freedom dues"—a new set of clothes, some food, farming implements, and 50 acres (approximately 20 hectares) of land. For many, this was more than they could ever expect to obtain in England, even with a lifetime of work. It made the years of harsh, forced labor and the chance of early death from disease or overwork well worth the risk.

English colonist Edward Waterhouse included this list of provisions to ensure survival in the New World with his *Relation of the Barbarous Massacre and A Declaration of the State of the Colony and Affaires in Virginia*, which was sent to England after the 1622 massacre. Among the list of items and prices are food, the most expensive, and a suit of armor.

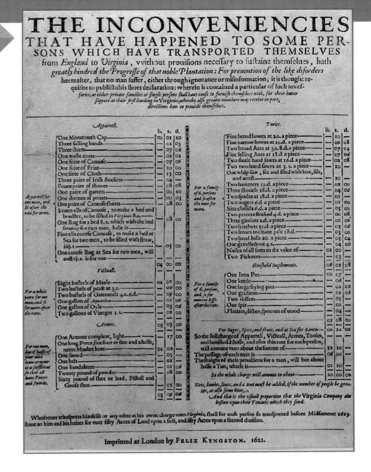

Most of these colonists were young males between the ages of fifteen and twenty-four. In the seventeenth century in Virginia, male colonists outnumbered female colonists by an average ratio ranging from 4 to 1 to 6 to 1. Females of childbearing age were so highly prized that some men in England sold their wives to recruiters for the Virginia Company. Abduction of females for shipment to Virginia—an act known as "trapanning" or "snaring"—was common enough to be the subject of folk ballads, such as "The Trapanned Maiden." Children were also so often kidnapped for shipment to Virginia that in 1645, the British parliament heard testimony about the practice. Those convicted of petty crimes, meanwhile, were subject to being "lagged"—forcibly shipped to Virginia as punishment.

This is a painting of a reconstruction of the settlement of Jamestown, as the fort most likely appeared in 1607. There was a broad swamp that surrounded the original settlement (the James River is pictured here in the foreground). This was advantageous for defense in case of attacks by the neighboring Native Americans but harmful for the health of the colonists because it attracted mosquitoes that carried malaria and was filled with waste that carried dysentery and typhus. Shortly after becoming a crown colony, Jamestown grew into New Town in the east. There are no written accounts of the original fort after the mid-1620s.

The Headright System

Land in Virginia was distributed according to what was called the headright system. Anyone who could pay his own passage to Virginia was given 50 acres of land (20 ha) on arrival and 50 acres (20 ha) more for each person—usually an indentured servant—whose passage they paid. Those who could afford to pay for their own passage were most often younger sons of the landowning classes or what were known as distressed cavaliers.

Pictured here is Sir Dudley Digges (1583–1639). He was a member of Parliament as well as a Virginia adventurer. Adventurers were those who invested in the Virginia Company, risking their capital. His son Edward was a Virginia planter and served as governor of the colony from 1655 to 1656. Edward Digges also set up the E. D. Plantation, which was known for its quality tobacco.

Younger Sons

Under English law and traditional custom, the eldest son of a landowner inherited all of the family's property upon the death of the father, leaving it necessary for younger sons to seek other opportunities. Many of these younger sons sought to make their fortune in Virginia. Many of the most prominent landowning families in Virginia were founded by these younger sons.

Distressed Cavaliers

Equally prominent as the founders of the first great Virginia estates were the group known as distressed cavaliers. These, too, were specifically targeted for recruitment by Governor William Berkeley in the mid-seventeenth century. The distressed cavaliers were members of noble families who had lost their property, title, and status. This loss was a result of backing the losing (Royalist) side in the civil war between supporters of the British monarchy and the backers of

Parliament in the mid-seventeenth century. They sought to re-create in Virginia the life of wealth, privilege, and ease that they had known and lost in England. Like the Virginia colonists from the lower classes, the younger sons and distressed cavaliers tended to be from the south and west of England.

Loose, Vagrant People and Wandering Savages

Common origins, however, did not necessarily make for any better relationship between the servant and the landowning classes in Virginia than it did in England. Discipline on the new estates in Virginia was harsh and physical. Labor was often extracted by the application of the whip and other violent punishments. Indentured servants in Virginia had few rights; they were little better than property, and their contracts could be sold, bartered, and even exchanged among landowners to settle debts. To the landowners, the servant class in Virginia was made up of nothing more than "loose, vagrant people, vicious and destitute of a means to live at home."

Violence also characterized the relations between the colonists and the native peoples of Virginia. At the time of the first English settlements along the Chesapeake, the region was home to about 24,000 Native Americans from thirty different Algonquian tribes, loosely united under the leadership of a chief named Powhatan. The colonists saw these Native Americans as obstacles to settlement that needed to be removed. They justified their attitudes by arguing that the Native Americans were "savages" and "barbarians." A Virginia settler named William Simmonds characterized them in a letter as "an idle, improvident, scattered people, ignorant of the knowledge of gold, or silver, or any commodities; and careless of anything but living from hand to mouth."

CHAPTER 5

Smoking tobacco was a "custom loathsome to the eye, hateful to the nose, harmful to the brain, [and] dangerous to the lung." wrote King James I in his 1604 essay "A Counterblast to Tobacco." Nonetheless, ever since Columbus had brought New World tobacco back with him from his first voyage, Europeans had not been able to get enough of it.

A Loathsome Habit, a Rich Crop

In 1616, John Rolfe of the Virginia Company discovered that the Chesapeake region was ideal for growing the crop. Tobacco thrives in a long, hot, humid growing season, and Virginia had just that. In addition, the numerous waterways of the Chesapeake Bay allowed the ships that would carry the product to England to sail almost up to the door of some plantations.

Land and Labor

By the 1620s, tobacco sold in England for ten times what it cost to grow in Virginia, even after factoring in the cost of shipping the product across the Atlantic Ocean. Tobacco was often used as currency in the colony. All that was necessary to make a fortune in Virginia, it seemed, was land and labor.

There was plenty of land available, especially once the Native Americans were routed from their traditional homes. As the number of Native Americans was diminishing, the number of colonists kept growing, despite the high death rate, from just 350 in 1616 to 13,500 less than thirty-five years later.

This contract of indentured servitude describes the terms and conditions for a young Virginian man named Thomas Clayton to apprentice himself to James Griffin, a woodworker, for five years beginning October 9, 1745. Thomas Clayton's father is deceased, but Clayton has gained his mother's permission for the indenture. By 1700, indentured servitude was no longer the dominant labor system in Virginia. By 1800 it was considered an insignificant labor system in the United States, although it continued as late as the 1830s. See a transcription of this image on page 55.

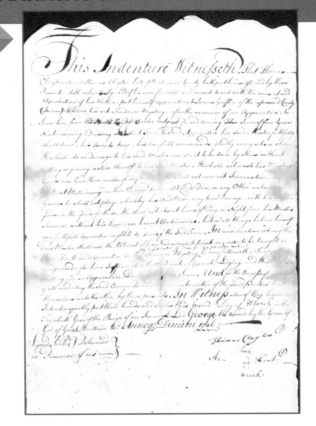

The Native Americans had no right to the land, the colonists maintained, because they had done nothing to "improve" it in the style that the English recognized, such as by building permanent homes and villages. "Our first work," wrote Sir Francis Wyatt, one of the colony's first governors, in a report to England, "is expulsion of the savages . . . " The English, said John Smith, had the right to take the land from the Native Americans because they had left Virginia "overgrown with trees and weeds, being a plain wilderness as God first made it."

And a wilderness, according to the English, belonged to anyone willing to claim and work it. By 1616, the English in Virginia had found good reason to work that wilderness. There was no gold or silver in Virginia, but, as the colonists discovered, the land was perfect for growing something worth almost as much: tobacco.

I·G Best VIRGINIA

Virginians exported 2,300 pounds of tobacco to England between 1615 and 1616. By the 1660s, Virginians were sending ten million pounds of tobacco to England. This "I.G. Best Virginia" is a tobacco label printed from a woodblock. The English bragged on the labels with verses such as the following: *Life is a smoke!—If this be true, Tobacco will thy life renew; Then fear not Death, nor killing care; Whilst we have best Virginia here.*

By 1669, the Native American population in the Chesapeake region had fallen from 24,000 to 2,000, and those that remained were begging for relief, both from the hostility of the colonists and from the depredations of the colonists' animals, which overran the Native Americans' land and destroyed their crops. "Your Hogs & Cattle injure us," begged a Native American petition in 1666. "We can [run] no further. Let us know where to live & how to be secured for the future from the Hogs & Cattle."

Chesapeake Houses

The lands vacated by the Native Americans were quickly settled by colonists. Most settlers cleared only about a tenth of their land, leaving the rest forested or as pasture for cattle.

Small tobacco planters in Virginia lived on their plots in what came to be known as Chesapeake houses, simple wooden constructions, 16 feet by 20 feet (4.9 by 6.1 m), without windows or foundations. Such houses consisted of two rooms on the dirt ground floor—a kitchen and a common room—with a sleeping loft under the eaves. Furniture consisted of little more than a single bed, a table, a bench, and possibly a chest for clothes. Some houses would not even have a bed but piles of straw or leaves to sleep on instead. The most common meal was a boiled porridge made of corn, peas, beans, and pork, with water or cider as the most common beverage. It was not a particularly fancy way of life, but it had several advantages over life in England. Unlike their counterparts in the lower classes in England, most Virginia colonists always had more than enough to eat. They also owned their own land, which made them independent and masterless, with little fear of having to answer to any authority for their freedom.

Slavery

Richer planters lived much more luxuriously, of course, in grand houses made of wood and modeled after country homes in the west of England. The truly rich built themselves homes of brick, which was regarded as the ultimate status symbol. Over time, such plantations became virtually self-sufficient. They raised all their own food in addition to the cash crop of tobacco. The plantations housed and fed virtually all necessary labor, including

RUN away from the subscriber, in *Chesterfield*, about the end of *August* last, a middle sized Negro man named WILL, about 30 years old, of a yellowish complexion, very much marked on his face, arms, and breast, his country fashion, speaks very broken, and can hardly tell his master's name; had on when he went away a new osnabrugs shirt, *Virginia* linen short trousers, old cotton jacket, and felt hat, with part of the brim burnt off. He has made three attempts, as he said, to get to his country, but was apprehended. All masters of vessels are hereby forewarned from carrying the said slave out of the colony. Whoever apprehends him, and brings him to me, shall have 20 s. reward, besides what the law allows. JORDAN ANDERSON.

This ad appeared in the *Virginia Gazette* on November 3, 1768. It includes the physical description of a runaway slave named Will, gives a warning to any "vessels" that may carry him out of the colony, and describes the reward that Jordan Anderson (the owner) will give to whomever returns him. In 1625, there were only 23 blacks in Virginia. By 1650, there were 300. By 1691, Virginia planters were prohibited from freeing slaves, unless they paid for the freed slave's transportation beyond the colony. By 1700, more than 1,000 Africans were arriving in the colony every year to work the plantations.

carpenters, blacksmiths, coopers, and grooms, as well as the large numbers of necessary field hands.

The way of life of such Virginia planters depended on huge amounts of labor. By the late seventeenth century, emigration from England was no longer sufficient to fill these needs. By 1700, virtually all of these laborers on the plantations were black slaves imported from Africa, and slavery had become the linchpin of the Virginia economy. Better economic conditions in England had reduced the number of men willing to emigrate to

Virginia as indentured servants. Planters increasingly saw little benefit in paying the passage of a servant whose labor they would enjoy only for four to seven years when they could own a slave for life. In 1650, there were only 300 slaves in Virginia. By 1700, that number had risen to 13,000. By 1750, it would rise to 150,000—40 percent of Virginia's population of 375,000 people.

A Reckless Extravagance

As Virginia became increasingly dependent on slavery, the way of life on its plantations was characterized by extravagance, largesse, recklessness, courtesy, and violence. These were seen by the planters as expressions of unchecked independence.

Rich Virginia planters prided themselves on their hospitality to any and all visitors. They dined and entertained on a scale that outsiders found difficult to believe. In a single year, one Virginia plantation house consumed 27,000 pounds (13,300 kilograms) of pork, 20 cattle, 350 bushels of wheat, four hogsheads (252 to 560 gallons, or approximately 93 to 201 dekaliters) of rum, and 150 gallons (68 dal) of brandy. In the winter, 28 separate fires were kept burning, requiring 6 oxen to haul the wood to the plantation house every day. Virginia planters were famous for living this way even when, as often happened, such reckless extravagance plunged them hopelessly into debt. When, after the American Revolution (1775–1783), Britain tallied the debt owed its merchants from the thirteen colonies, half of that debt came from Virginia. The largest individual debtor was Thomas Jefferson.

Male Virginians of the upper classes prided themselves on exquisite manners, elaborate courtesy, a volatile temperament, and high spirits. Characteristic of a Virginia gentleman was his mastery of "condescension," which a modern historian, Alan

This is a portrait of Lucy Randolph Burwell (1744–1802), who belonged to one of Virginia's wealthiest families. She is wearing the very latest fashion of the day and idly playing a guitarlike instrument. Lucy Randolph married Lewis Burwell, who was from a neighboring plantation. Virginia's ruling elite intermarried to enhance their social status and diminish any questionable reputation or lower-class origins their grandparents may have had. Women in Virginia were expected to be refined, feminine, gracious, modest, and delicate.

Taylor, in his book *American Colonies*, defines as "a gentleman's ability to treat common people affably without sacrificing any sense of superiority."

Condescension did not extend to slaves, however. Virginians often lamented the need for treating their human property with the "severity" necessary to extract obedience and labor from them. They prized the ability to act with sufficient brutality when required. Upper-class Virginians also congratulated themselves for their sense of honor, a sometimes exaggerated sense of their own dignity often defended with duels or other outbursts of violence. Such volatile high spirits were regarded as a sign of masculinity. Gambling, horse racing, and hunting were the favorite pastimes of male Virginians of all classes. As the slave population of Virginia grew, this heightened sense of honor and independence among white Virginians became an increasingly important element of their identity.

CHAPTER 6

Most Virginians had always had reason to distrust government, going back either to their own or to their ancestors'
days in England. Members of the English aristocracy had good reason to consider themselves freer than other Europeans. But for
the lower classes, the government was mainly an instrument of
oppression. All that they might know of the
government was that it taxed them, passed
all kinds of laws that could be used against
them, and used vagrancy statutes to limit
their mobility.

If This
Be Treason

The distressed cavaliers who came to
Virginia also had reason to distrust govern-
ment, at least parliamentary government.
The reason they left England was that the form of government
they supported—the monarchy—had been overthrown by
Parliament and its supporters. The experience left many with bit-
ter feelings toward the British government and especially toward
Parliament.

Self-Government in Virginia

Virginians insisted on a large degree of self-government almost
from the colony's beginnings. From 1619 onward, Virginia was
run, as would be most of the other American colonies, by a governor, who was appointed by the British government; a council,
whose members were also appointed by the government; and an
assembly of representatives, whose members were elected by the
Virginians themselves. (One had to be a white adult male and a
property owner in order to vote.) This assembly was known as

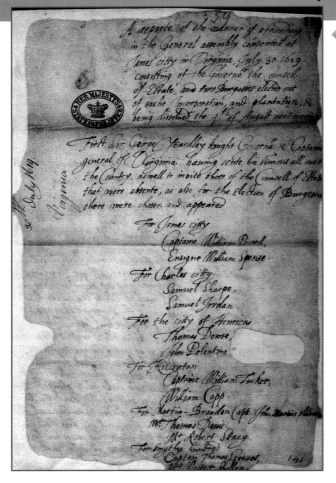

This is a list of burgesses elected to the first assembly at Jamestown—the first such assembly to take place on the American continent. The twenty-two elected burgesses met in July and August 1619, where they passed measures against public drunkenness, idleness, and gambling, as well as a measure requiring church attendance. The first poll tax was also approved, requiring these officers to be paid "one pound of the best Tobacco for their service during that hot, humid midsummer session."

the House of Burgesses, and it was the first elected representative assembly in the American colonies.

Taxation

The governor, who was considered the British crown's direct representative in Virginia, wielded tremendous power. He could, for instance, reward his supporters with land grants, and he could veto any measure passed by the House of Burgesses.

William Berkeley was the most influential of Virginia's governors. He served from 1642 to 1652, and again from 1660 to 1677. He was largely responsible for recruiting the cavaliers who came to Virginia as colonists. But the House of Burgesses had tremendous power of its own. From its beginnings, it claimed for itself the sole right to pass tax measures for the colony. This meant that the Virginians themselves, as represented by the burgesses, controlled the raising and spending of public money in the colony.

The representative assemblies in other colonies would claim this same right for themselves. It was this right, more than anything else, that the colonists were concerned about when they insisted on self-government.

Towns and Counties

In other important ways, government in Virginia differed greatly from government in a colony such as Massachusetts. In Massachusetts, the colonists settled close together, in compact towns. The most important institution of local government was the town, and the primary agency of government was the town meeting. In town meetings, the adult males of the town would gather several times a year to discuss and vote on matters of importance.

Virginians lived far apart from each other due to the great size of the tobacco plantations and homesteads. There were few towns and few town meetings. The most important institution of local government was the county, and all-important local business was conducted at the county courthouse. On court days, anyone with business to conduct, as well as the merely curious and assorted hangers-on, came by horseback, often from long distances, to the courthouse. Court day was therefore a time for pleasure as well as business, as people exchanged gossip, played cards, and otherwise found diversions on which to spend their time. A highlight of most court days would be horse racing, with enthusiastic betting by participants and onlookers.

Freedom from Government

By "self-government," most Virginians meant freedom from government interference in or regulation of their lives. Above all, they meant freedom from taxes, particularly taxes they had not imposed upon themselves. They were quick to assert themselves when they felt government had overstepped its bounds.

Bacon's Rebellion

By the 1670s, many Virginians, particularly smaller planters on the colony's frontier, had grown impatient with Berkeley's high-handed rule, which they felt consistently favored the larger planters and the cavaliers. They were also angry that Berkeley restrained them from attacking the Native Americans, believing that the governor acted in this way because he was personally profiting from trading furs with the frontier tribes.

In 1676, under the leadership of a rich, young lawyer named Nathaniel Bacon, they rose in armed rebellion against the governor and his supporters. They marched on the colony's capital, Jamestown, and drove the governor away. But when Bacon died of a fever, the rebellion fizzled. Berkeley regained control of the colony. In reprisal, he hanged twenty-three of the revolt's ringleaders. At this point, even the British crown believed he had gone too far, and he was relieved of his post.

Discontent with Britain

Decisions made in London, the British capital, aroused more permanent resentments among Virginians. Discontent began as early as 1644. In that year, Britain imposed the Navigation Act, which declared that Virginians could only sell their tobacco to

This engraving by H. B. Hall depicts Patrick Henry addressing the House of Burgesses on May 30, 1765. Henry passionately speaks against the Stamp Act, which lies crumpled on the floor behind him, as his fellow burgesses intently listen. At the time, Henry was the newly elected burgess from the county of Louisa. As a child, Henry was taught at home by his father. John taught Henry such subjects as Latin. Henry later taught himself law. His fight against British tyranny in every movement for colonial rights is Patrick Henry's lasting legacy.

Britain, could only ship their tobacco in British ships, and in general could trade only with Britain. The act marked the beginnings of a rupture in the relationship between Virginians and their mother country.

The final break came, of course, in 1776, with the decision of the thirteen colonies to declare their independence from Britain. Virginia was in the forefront of the independence movement, firing what many historians consider to be the figurative first shot of the American Revolution as early as 1765.

In 1763, Great Britain had emerged victorious from a global war with France over colonies, but it was also nearly bankrupt. As a solution to Britain's financial woes, Parliament and the king decided that the country could gain revenue by directly taxing the American colonies. This infringed directly on the colonists' prized right of self-government. What followed was a series of British laws that levied taxes on everything from sugar to tea to tobacco and even virtually all printed material—the colonists referred to these laws collectively as the Intolerable Acts.

By the 1760s, an increasingly smaller number of Virginians had direct memories of life in Great Britain. For most Virginians, their contact with Britain was limited to the taxes they were now being made to pay. The colony's most important contact with Britain was economic, in the form of trade. When Britain passed the Stamp Act in 1765, opposition in Virginia was particularly fierce.

A day after his twenty-ninth birthday, a recently elected member of the House of Burgesses, Patrick Henry, gave a speech in the House. He opposed the act, asserting that only colonial assemblies had the right to tax the colonies. An inspired orator, Henry owed his popularity and election as a burgess to a fiery speech he'd given two years earlier in which he argued that King George III had forfeited any right to loyalty and obedience from the colonies.

On this day, he went even further. Referring to the king, he proclaimed, "Caesar had his Brutus, Charles the First his Cromwell, and George the III . . ." At that point, he was interrupted by shocked cries of "treason" from some of the burgesses. This was further than even the most rebellious of them had dared to go. Henry's allusions were to monarchs who had been assassinated because of their abuse of power; his listeners realized that he was apparently about to call for the assassination of Britain's king. "Treason, treason!" the

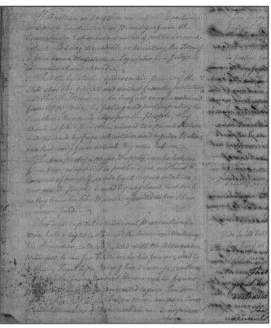

George Mason (1725–1792) was elected to the Virginia House of Burgesses in 1759. In 1776, he penned most of Virginia's Declaration of Rights, with Thomas Ludwell adding several additional clauses. The first draft of this document, which would serve as Jefferson's model when writing the Declaration of Independence, is pictured here. Mason attended the Constitutional Convention in Philadelphia in 1787. Toward the end of the convention, he surprisingly decided not to sign the Constitution. He sighted many concerns, including the lack of a declaration of rights. His concern brought about the creation of the Bill of Rights.

cries ran out, but Henry continued on, undeterred. "And George the Third may profit from their example," he said, before adding, "If this be treason, make the most of it."

Henry's rebellious eloquence convinced the House of Burgesses to pass a resolution denouncing the Stamp Act, which was immediately circulated among the other colonies, inspiring them to their own acts of defiance. As the crisis deepened, leading to the colonies' final break with England, Virginians were among the most important leaders. Henry continued to inspire the colonists with his oratory, winning even greater renown for a speech in which he passionately declared, "Give me liberty, or give me death." A wealthy, scholarly Virginia landowner, writer, and scientist, Thomas Jefferson, penned the immortal words of the Declaration of Independence, which articulated the colonists' grievances and continue to inspire liberty around the world. Virginia's biggest landowner, wealthiest man, and most respected citizen, George Washington, became the commander in chief of the colonists' forces and later became the first president of the victorious United States. James Madison, a tiny, brilliant friend of the towering Jefferson, wrote much of the Constitution. Numerous Virginians, prominent and not, fought for the Continental army. The final battle of the war, at Yorktown, was fought on Virginia soil in 1781. Of the thirteen colonies, none played a bigger role in the events that created the independent United States of America than the first to be established—Virginia.

TIMELINE

1497 —— England's first claim to North America is established when John Cabot lands on the shores of the New World.

1585 —— Sir Walter Raleigh arrives at Roanoke Island. This area is named Virginia for Queen Elizabeth I of England. The colony established here survives for only one year.

1587 —— A second attempt is made to establish Roanoke Island, Virginia (which is now North Carolina), as a colony. This fails, and the colony mysteriously disappears by 1590. This is now known as the Lost Colony.

1606 —— King James of England grants a charter to the London Company (later called the Virginia Company) for a new colonizing expedition to the New World. The London Company launches its first expedition, and three ships set sail from England.

1607 —— The three ships arrive in Virginia on May 14. The first permanent English settlement in the New World is named Jamestown.

1609 —— The king of England transfers control and governance of the Virginia colony from the British crown to the London company.

1619 —— The first legislative assembly, called the House of Burgesses, is formed in the Virginia colony. The first black slaves arrive in Virginia.

1624 —— The Virginia Company governs the colony for seventeen years, until King James I cancels the company charter and Virginia becomes a royal province. Except for the years of English commonwealth, Virginia remains under royal rule until 1776.

1650 —— The colonists defeat the Powhatan Indians after battling with them off and on for forty-four years. The death rate in the Virginia colony declines after this fight.

1651 —— In these years, the Navigation Acts are passed by
–1673 Parliament. The 1651 act requires that all imports to England must be shipped only on British ships. The 1659 act states that colonists can only ship products to England. The 1673 act establishes that duties must be paid on goods that pass between plantations. These acts created economic hardships that led to unrest in the colonies.

1676 —— Nathaniel Bacon leads Bacon's Rebellion against Governor William Berkeley. Jamestown is burned to the ground. The rebellion ends when Bacon suddenly dies in October.

1698 —— Jamestown is burned again.

1699 —— The capital of Virginia is moved to Williamsburg. Jamestown is no longer a city.

1764 —— Various tax acts on items such as tea, sugar, and
-1773 stamps are passed by Parliament to levy taxes on the colonies. In 1766, the Declaratory Act is passed, declaring supremacy over American colonies "in all cases whatsoever." Colonists rebel against these attempts to establish control over the colonies.

1774 —— The First Continental Congress issues a declaration and resolve, which asserts the rights of colonists and colonial assemblies.

1775 —— The Revolutionary War begins.

1776 —— The Declaration of Independence is adopted by the Second Continental Congress on July 4, and the United States of America is born.

1781 —— The British surrender on October 19, 1781. The Treaty of Paris is signed in 1783, ending the Revolutionary War.

PRIMARY SOURCE TRANSCRIPTIONS

Page 20: The title page of *The New Life of Virginea*

Transcription
The New Life of Virginia, Declaring the Former Success and Present State of that plantation, being the second part of Nova Britannia.

Published by the authority of his Majesties Counsel of Virginia, London.

Imprinted by Felix Kyngston for William Welby, dwelling at the sign of the Swan in Paul's Churchyard, 1612.

Page 21: Excerpt from *The New Life of Virginea*

Transcription
. . . And if any man asks, what benefit can this plantation be to them that be no Adventurers therein . . . ? First, we say, (setting aside their possibility of prize) what man so simple that does not see the necessity of employment for our multitude of people? Which though they be our flourishing fruits of peace and health, yet be they no longer good and wholesome in themselves, then either our domestic or foreign actions can make them profitable, or not hurtful to the Commonwealth.

. . . And as it is impossible without this course of sending out the offspring of our families, in so great a body of many millions, which yearly do increase amongst us, to prevent their manifold diseases of poverty, corruption of mind, and pestilent infection, so the burden thereof in some proportion is felt by every man in his private calling, either in the tax of their maintenance and daily relief, or in the taint of their vices and bodily plagues. And by this means only it may soon be eased, to the sensible good of every man, as in the greater safety and freedom from infection, so in the price and plenty of all outward and necessary things.

Page 27: Title page of *The Generall Historie* **by Captain John Smith**

Transcription
The General History of Virginia, New England, and the Summer Isles: with the names of the Adventurers, Planters, and Governors from their first beginning Year 1584 to this present 1624.

With the proceedings of those several colonies and the Accidents that befell them in all their journeys and discoveries.

Also the maps and descriptions of all those countries, their commodities, people, government, customs, and religion yet known.

Divided into six books. By Captain John Smith, journeyman, governor, in those countries of Admiral of New England.

London. Printed by I.D. and L.H. for Michael Sparkes. 1624

Page 27: Excerpt from *The Generall Historie* by Captain John Smith, book three, chapter two, in which Smith describes being rescued by Pocahontas. (Smith refers to himself in third person.)

Transcription
At his entrance before the King, all the people gave a great shout. The Queen of Appomattoc was appointed to bring him water to wash his hands, and another brought him a bunch of feathers, instead of a towel, to dry them; having feasted him after their best barbarous manner they could, a long consultation was held, but the conclusion was, two great stones were brought before Powhatan; then as many as could laid hands on him, dragged him to them, and there on laid his head and being ready with their clubs to beat out his brains, Pocahontas, the kings' dearest daughter, when no entreaty could prevail, got his head in her arms and laid her own upon his to save him from death, whereat the Emperor was contented he should live to make him hatchets, and her bells, beads, and copper, for they thought him as well of all occupations as themselves . . .

Page 35: Contract of Indenture of Thomas Clayton

Transcription
This Indenture witnesseth, that Thomas Clayton, son of Thomas Clayton late of Richmond County hath put himself, and by these presents, doth voluntarily, and of his own free will and accord, to and with the consent and approbation of his mother, put himself apprentice to James Griffin of the aforesaid county (Joiner), to learn his art and trade, or mystery, after the manner of an apprentice; to serve him from the ninth day of October last past, for and during the term of five years next ensuing; during which term the said apprentice his said Master faithfully shall serve, his secrets keep, his lawful commands gladly everywhere obey. He shall do no damage to his said Master, nor see it to be done by others without letting or giving notice thereof, to his said Master. He shall not waste his Master's goods nor lend them unlawfully to any. He shall not commit fornication, nor contract matrimony

within the said term. At cards, dice, or any other unlawful games he shall not play, whereby his said Master may have damage, with his own goods or the goods of others. He shall not absent himself day or night from his Master's service without his leave, nor haunt ordinaries, but in all things behave himself as a faithful apprentice ought to do during the said term. In consideration whereof the said Master shall use the utmost of his endeavour to teach or cause to be taught or instructed, the said apprentice in the trade or mystery of a joiner and house painter which he now followeth; and procure and provide for him sufficient meal, drink, apparel, lodging, and washing fitting for an apprentice during the said term, and for the performance of all and every the said covenants and agreements, either of the said parties bind themselves unto the other by these presents. In witness whereof they have interchangeably put their hands and seales this proud day of March in the twentieth year of the reign of our Sovereign Lord George the second by the Grace of God of Great Brittain. Anno Domini 1746.

Signed, Sealed and Delivered
In the Presence of Us
Thomas Clayton
Ann Hunt

GLOSSARY

accolade An award or expression of praise.

affably Pleasantly.

anarchy The absence of government, laws, and any other established order.

burgess A citizen of a British borough, or a representative of a borough or county.

charter A document issued by a governing body that grants rights to a corporation.

cooper A person who repairs wooden barrels or casks.

countinghouse An accounting office.

dysentery An infection in the intestines that causes severe diarrhea.

eaves The lower part of a roof that overhangs the wall.

estuary A passage of water where the river and sea meet.

Federalist Papers A series of articles published in circulating colonial newspapers from 1787 to 1788 under the pen name Publius. They were written by Alexander Hamilton, John Jay, and James Madison. The articles' purpose was to gain support for the proposed written constitution.

gibbet The gallows, or a wooden instrument of execution where the condemned person is hanged.

groom A person who tends to horses.

harbinger A precursor or foreshadowing of an event to come.

homestead The home and land occupied by a family.

incipient To begin to become evident; to come into being.

largesse Generosity.

linchpin A person or situation that serves as an anchor or foundation to the success of something.

malaria An infectious disease caused by parasites carried by a certain type of mosquito. Symptoms include chills and fever.

orator A person who delivers a speech.

plunder Something taken by force.

porridge A soft food made by boiling meal with milk or water until thick.

profusion A great quantity or supply; extravagance.

Reformation The movement that took place in the sixteenth century to reform the Catholic Church and that resulted in the establishment of Protestant churches.

reprisal An act of retaliation for wrongdoing.

schism The division or separation from a church or other religious body.

treason The betrayal of a ruler or government.

typhus A group of bacterial diseases that can be spread to humans by fleas and body lice. Symptoms include high fever, headache, and rash.

FOR MORE INFORMATION

The Colonial Williamsburg Foundation
P. O. Box 1776
Williamsburg, VA 23187-1776
(757) 229-1000
http://www.colonialwilliamsburg.org

Monticello and the Thomas Jefferson Foundation
P. O. Box 316
Charlottesville, VA 22902
http://www.monticello.org/index.html

Virginia Historical Society
P.O. Box 7311
Richmond, VA 23221-0311
(804) 358-4901
http://www.vahistorical.org

Web Sites

Due to the changing nature of Internet links, the Rosen Publishing Group, Inc., has developed an online list of Web sites related to the subject of this book. This site is updated regularly. Please use this link to access the list:

http://www.rosenlinks.com/pstc/virg

FOR FURTHER READING

Carson, Mary Kay. *Colonial America*. New York, NY: Scholastic, 1999.

Doak, Robin S. *Smith: John Smith and the Settlement of Jamestown* (Exploring the World). Minneapolis, MN: Compass Point Books, 2003.

Harness, Cheryl. *Thomas Jefferson*. New York, NY: National Geographic, 2004.

Murray, Aaron R. *American Revolution Battles and Leaders*. New York, NY: DK Publishers Inc., 2004.

Sakurai, Gayle. *The Thirteen Colonies* (Cornerstones of Freedom). Danbury, CT: Children's Press, 2000.

BIBLIOGRAPHY

Bailyn, Bernard. *The Peopling of North America: An Introduction.* New York, NY: Vintage, 1992.

Byrd, William. *Histories of the Dividing Line Betwixt Virginia and North Carolina.* New York, NY: Dover, 1987.

Fisher, David Hackett. *Albion's Seed: Four British Folkways in America.* New York, NY: Oxford University Press, 1991.

Galeano, Eduardo. *Open Veins of Latin America: Five Centuries of the Pillage of a Continent.* New York, NY: Vintage, 1998.

Greenblatt, Stephen. *Will in the World: How Shakespeare Became Shakespeare.* New York, NY: W. W. Norton, 2004.

Hofstadter, Richard. *America at 1750: A Social Portrait.* New York, NY: Vintage, 1973.

Jefferson, Thomas. *Writings.* New York, NY: Library of America, 1984.

Taylor, Alan. *American Colonies* (The Penguin History of the United States). New York, NY: Penguin, 2002.

Zinn, Howard. *A People's History of the United States: 1492–Present.* New York, NY: Perennial, 2003.

PRIMARY SOURCE IMAGE LIST

Cover: Theodor de Bry's (1528–1598) engraving titled *Captain Gosnold Trades with Indians, Virginia*, 1634, located at the British Library, London, England.

Page 6 (left): *George Washington, Athenaeum* by Gilbert Stuart, circa 1810. Housed at the Museum of Fine Arts, Boston, Massachusetts.

Page 6 (right): *Portrait of James Madison* by Chester Harding (1792–1866). Housed at the National Portrait Gallery, Smithsonian Institution.

Page 6 (bottom): *Portrait of President Thomas Jefferson* by Rembrandt Peale, created in 1800. Owned by the White House Historical Association (White House Collection).

Page 9 (left): Portrait of Queen Mary I of England by Sir Anthonis Mor (1517/20–1567/7). Housed at Hever Castle, Ltd., Kent, England.

Page 9 (right): Portrait of Queen Elizabeth I, circa 1585–1590, by John Bettes, the Younger. Housed at Hever Castle Ltd., Kent, England.

Page 10: *Die Societas Jesu in Europa, 1643–1644* from Mathias Tanner, Rare Books and Special Collections Division, Library of Congress.

Page 11: *The Bible and Holy Scriptures Conteyned in the Olde and Newe Testament*, Geneva, 1560. Housed at the Rare Books and Special Collections Division, Library of Congress.

Page 15: *Augustine par Floridae* by Baptista Boazio, London, 1589. Part of the Drake Collection in the Rare Books and Special Collections Division, Library of Congress.

Page 19: Woodcut of beggar tied and whipped through the streets, circa 1567. Part of a private collection courtesy of the Bridgeman Art Library, London, England.

Page 20: Title page of *The New Life of Virginea*, printed in London in 1612 by Felix Kyngston for William Welby. Part of the University of Glasgow's Library Special Collections Americana Exhibition.

Page 23 (left): *Indian Village of Pomeiooc,* watercolor drawing by John White, created 1585–1586. Housed in the British Museum, London, England.

Page 23 (right): *Indian in Body Paint,* watercolor drawing by John White, created 1585–1586. Housed in the British Museum, London, England.

Page 24: *Americae Pars, Nunc Virginia Dicta*, 1590, by Theodor de Bry based on drawings by John White. A copy is housed at the American Memory Collection, Library of Congress, Geography and Map Division.

Page 27 (left): Portrait of Captain John Smith circa 1616, oil on canvas. Part of a private collection courtesy of the Bridgeman Art Library, London, England.

Page 27 (right): The title page of *The Generall Historie of Virginia, New-England, and the Summer Isles* by Captain John Smith. Part of the Rare Books & Manuscripts Collection, New York Public Library, Astor, Lenox, and Tilden Foundations.

Page 28: Charter of the Virginia Company of London, 1606. Jefferson Papers, American Memory Collection, Library of Congress.

Page 31: An abbreviated list printed in 1630 of "Needefull Things" for a Virginia Immigrant from Edward Waterhouse's *A Declaration of the State of the Colony and Affaires in Virginia* (1622). Housed at the British Library, London, England.

Page 33: Portrait of Sir Dudley Digges, painted by Cornelius Janssen in 1636. Owned by the Virginia Historical Society.

Page 35: Indenture contract of Thomas Clayton. Housed at the Colonial Williamsburg Foundation.

Page 37: "I.G. Best Virginia" tobacco label from engraved printing woodblock (late seventeenth through nineteenth centuries). Owned by the Virginia Historical Society.

Page 39: Runaway slave ad from the *Virginia Gazette*, 1768. Housed at the Colonial Williamsburg Foundation: John D. Rockefeller, Jr. Library.

Page 41: Portrait of Lucy Randolph Burwell, circa 1773, most likely painted by Matthew Pratt. Housed at the Virginia Historical Society.

Page 44: List of burgesses elected to the first assembly at "James City" (Jamestown), Virginia, 1619. Part of the Public Record Office of the National Archives of the United Kingdom. Topham-HIP Photo Archives.

Page 49 (right): George Mason's Virginia Declaration of Rights, 1776. Manuscript Division, Library of Congress.

INDEX

About the Author

Sandra Whiteknact is a writer, artist, educator, and activist. She hopes that teaching young readers about colonial America's "great experiment" will inspire their interest in the meaning of true democracy.

Photo Credits

Cover HIP/Scala/Art Resource, NY; p. 1 Private Collection/Bridgeman Art Library; p. 6 (top left) © Museum of the City of New York/Corbis; p. 6 (top right) National Portrait Gallery, Smithsonian Institution/Art Resource, NY; p. 6 (bottom), 20, 49 (left) © Bettmann/Corbis; p. 9 (left and right) Hever Castle Ltd, Kent, UK/ Bridgeman Art Library; pp. 10, 11 Library of Congress, Rare Book and Special Collections Division; p. 15 Private Collection, Archives Charmet/Bridgeman Art Library; p. 18 Private Collection, The Stapleton Collection/Bridgeman Art Library; pp. 19, 27 (left) Private Collection/Bridgeman Art Library; p. 23 (left) Art Resource, NY; p. 23 (right) HIP/Art Resource, NY; p. 24 Library of Congress, Geography and Map Division; p. 27 (right) Rare Books and Manuscripts Collection, New York Public Library, Astor, Lenox, and Tilden Foundations; p. 28 1606, Virginia Records Time Line, 1553–1743, Jefferson Papers, American Memory Collections, Library of Congress; p. 31 The British Library; p. 32 © Bettmann/Corbis; p. 33 © 2005 Getty Images; pp. 35, 39 Special Collections, John D. Rockefeller Jr. Library, The Colonial Williamsburg Foundation; p. 37 New York Public Library, Humanities and Social Sciences Library/George Arents Collection; p. 41 The Virginia Historical Society, Richmond, Virginia; p. 44 © Public record Office/Topham-HIP/The Image Works; p. 47 © Art Resource, NY; p. 49 (right) Library of Congress, Manuscripts Division.

Editor: Leigh Ann Cobb